Dear Parent:

Buckle up! You are about to join your child on a very exciting journey. The destination? Independent reading!

Road to Reading will help you and your child get there. The program offers books at five levels, or Miles, that accompany children from their first attempts at reading to successfully reading on their own. Each Mile is paved with engaging stories and delightful artwork.

MILE 1 — Getting Started
For children who know the alphabet and are eager to begin reading
• easy words • fun rhythms • big type • picture clues

MILE 2 — Reading With Help
For children who recognize some words and sound out others with help
• short sentences • pattern stories • simple plotlines

MILE 3 — Reading On Your Own
For children who are ready to read easy stories by themselves
• longer sentences • more complex plotlines • easy dialogue

MILE 4 — First Chapter Books
For children who want to take the plunge into chapter books
• bite-size chapters • short paragraphs • full-color art

MILE 5 — Chapter Books
For children who are comfortable reading independently
• longer chapters • occasional black-and-white illustrations

There's no need to hurry through the Miles. Road to Reading is designed without age or grade levels. Children can progress at their own speed, developing confidence and pride in their reading ability no matter what their age or grade.

So sit back and enjoy the ride—every Mile of the way!

To Joshua, who loves books
N.S.L.

For Francesca
V.P.

Library of Congress Cataloging-in-Publication Data
Levinson, Nancy Smiler.
Say Cheese! / by Nancy Smiler Levinson ; illustrated by Valeria Petrone
   p. cm. — (Road to reading. Mile 1)
Summary: A monkey keeps trying to take a photograph of a giraffe couple, but the other animals insist on pushing their way into the picture.
ISBN 0-307-26110-7 (pbk)—ISBN 0-307-46110-6 (GB)
[1. Photography Fiction. 2. Monkeys Fiction. 3. Giraffes Fiction.
4. Animals Fiction.] I. Petrone, Valeria, ill.
II. Title.   III. Series.
PZ7.L5794Say 2000
[E]—DC21
99-24461
CIP

A GOLDEN BOOK • New York
Golden Books Publishing Company, Inc. New York, New York 10106

ISBN: 0-307-26110-7 (pbk)
ISBN: 0-307-46110-6 (GB)
Printed in the United States of America   12 11 10 9 8 7 6 5 4 3

SAY CHEESE!

BY NANCY SMILER LEVINSON
ILLUSTRATED BY VALERIA PETRONE

Ready?

Smile, please.
Say cheese.

Wait!

Smile, please.
Say cheese.

Wait!
Don't forget me!

Smile, please.
Say cheese.

And me!

And me!

Smile, please.
Say cheese.

Wait!

Don't forget...

Smile, please.
Say cheese.